A Manifesto of Radical Optimism

by

Dylan Brody

Also by Dylan Brody

BOOKS

Heroes Fall (a novella)
Laughs Last
The Warm Hello
A Tale of a Hero and the Song of her Sword
Xenophobia and the Jewish Druid

COMING SOON
Relatively Painless

CDs
True Enough
Brevity
A Twist of the Wit
Chronological Disorder
Write Large

All these and more available at http://dylanbrody.com

© 2020

All rights reserved. No part of this publication may be reproduced or transmitted in any form or by any means, electronic or mechanical, including photocopying or recording or by any information storage and retrieval systems, without express written consent of the author.

Copyright owned by Dylan Brody

Published April, 2020   Active Voice Productions

Foreword

by
Myq Kaplan

The world is full of suffering, we are ash and dust, and I am an optimist.

And this introduction is for pessimists.

If you think that nothing matters and nothing will change for the better, I get it. So why not spend some of your meaningless time reading this book?

You've already picked up the book. Why not read it? Couldn't hurt! And if it does hurt, doesn't that just continue to confirm your pessimistic world view that nothing can change for the better, and isn't that satisfying in a way?

Maybe the half-empty glass will become even emptier! (And wouldn't a true pessimist see the glass as COMPLETELY empty? Why stop at half? Empty that glass! You can do it! I'm optimistic for you.)

If you're a pessimist who thinks that even a book on optimism could only add fuel to your pessimistic fire, well then, wouldn't you like that? You get to keep being your pessimistic self, only even more so.

Now, if you're skeptical of me and Dylan and this book and the whole idea of optimism because how can you be an optimist when the world is full of suffering, I get it, and in fact this book is even MORE important for you to read.

Why?

Rabbi Simcha Bunim is credited with saying, "Everyone must have two pockets, with a note in each pocket, so that he or she can reach into one or the other, depending on the need. When feeling lowly and depressed, discouraged or disconsolate, one should reach into the right pocket, and, there, find the words: Bishvili nivra ha-olam 'The world was created for me.' But when feeling high and mighty one should reach into the left pocket and find the words: V'anochi afar v'efer 'I am but dust and ashes.'"

The glass is both half empty AND half full. There is fuel for any fire we want to feed.

There is a common misconception that optimism is about thinking things are good even when things are not. This book is not about just imagining that things are better than they are, fantasizing about a world in which everything is fair and just and merciful and kind. It is about so imagining, so fantasizing, and then taking action to head in the direction of those imaginations and fantasies. This book is about addressing the ash and dust, about creating a better world out of it, about offering a constructive, practical perspective on how we can do that. It's not pie in the sky. It's pie on the ground. Pie right here.

Ash and dust are not nothing. They are something. And they can become something else. With work and time. The way that stardust became us.

If you believe, and you act on that belief, and put in work, time, and effort, sometimes you can accomplish something, more than if you didn't do anything. I believe it because I've seen it, and done it, and seen people do it with less than I've started with. And more importantly, if you DON'T believe, and you DON'T put in any work, time, or effort, for sure you can definitely NOT accomplish something.

And if you think that reading the book will do nothing for you or the world, maybe you're right, but then why not read it to PROVE that you're right? Read it, see what it says, and if nothing improves ever, you win. But you can't win unless you read it. I can't promise magical results for society or your life, but I CAN promise that if you DON'T read it, there will be NO magical results.

You know that we're all ash and dust. Now also know that the world was created for us, and maybe more importantly, it is continually created BY us. We are creating this world RIGHT NOW. The world is coming from inside itself! From inside OURselves. We are creating it with the choices we make. The beliefs we act on. The steps we take. So, start with this small step (that you've already started taking, because you are doing it right now): READ THIS BOOK. Because for sure if we do nothing, we can for sure accomplish nothing. On that, I am very optimistic.

INTRODUCTION

As I type these words, I find myself in my home with my wife and dogs, anticipating a lengthy confinement. I have had the idea for this book for a long time. I began it. I asked a friend to write a foreword. I set it aside. I came back to it.

It is not an 'entertainment.' The idea for a Manifesto of Radical Optimism came to me not as a satirical, or comedic look at a topic. I resisted putting it to the page. The loftiness of the Big Idea felt beyond my authority. Who am I, a humorist who depends on the trick of getting laughs to earn the attention of strangers, to have philosophical thoughts and share them with the world? I feared that my fans might be disappointed to read something more serious. I hate to disappoint those nine people simultaneously. Also, it gave me a self-indulgent moment to imagine that there are many more.

As Covid-19 spreads terrifyingly in Italy and America has just begun to self-isolate and maintain social distancing, it feels catastrophe has befallen the species. The book feels increasingly urgent and with the urgency, I realize its actual value.

The underlying premises are simple:
- Societal despair paralyzes the people as depression paralyzes the individual sufferer
- An obsolete power structure, fearing change, has weaponized the levers of complacency and despair, dependence and despondency
- In times of profound, societal, viral, weaponized hopelessness and helplessness, optimism itself becomes a tool of radical action

This pandemic makes us feel helpless while it aligns nicely with our penchant for apocalyptic fantasy. This pandemic will not be an end. It will be, as all plagues, wars, and wide-reaching natural disasters have been since the beginning of the human struggle to survive, an inflection point in a long history.

There is much we have yet to see. How many will die? How long will the mitigation factors remain in place, the lock downs, the social distancing, the ZOOM calls, the closed diners, the twenty-four-hour news coverage, the bizarre narrative-shopping of the wholly incompetent executive branch, the toilet-paper hoarding? How will society function at the end of it all, when a world of under-educated children and bereaved adults stumbles out into an eventual new day of herd immunity or a newly vaccinated world of sunshine and blue skies? We have yet to see.

The world will not be as it was.

Internet friends and colleagues keep reminding one another that Shakespeare wrote *King Lear* while under quarantine for the bubonic plague. A good deal of Sir Isaac Newton's most important work reached the page when he was under a similar quarantine.

When I began this book, it was in response to a seemingly unassailable power structure and a cowed populace entertained into perpetually depressed submission. Our resentments, like those of a toddler toward a parent, revealed themselves in futile tantrums and inward-turned rages. We saw injustice, inequity, abuses of power, consolidation of wealth and we wanted change but did not know how to demand it.

After decades of cultural anti- intellectualism and undermining of public education we had become societally incapable of proper critical thought. Our sense of hope, aspiration and anticipation had been reduced to a Pavlovian response to the theme songs of our most soothing sitcoms and an emotional investment in the drunk housewives of various cities, whose choreographed antics celebrated upper-middleclass alcoholic drama as if it were an accomplishment of artistic merit.

Now, with the natural force of a virus spreading widely, the schism between the world we live in and the world we pretend to live in becomes apparent. We remember that we as individuals are small parts, each of us, of a vast species, a spreading force, virus-like within an ecosphere. We remember that we are each alone and that we are all together. We remember. We relearn.

As we look forward now, in this time of forced and discomfiting upheaval, let us think to the world beyond this moment. How might we utilize this crisis as an opportunity to reset some vital relationships while we are apart so that the world we emerge to might be brighter and better and healthier than the one we leave behind.

Dark ages end, sometimes with plague. If we guide the end of the dark age correctly, we can emerge to a new, bright renaissance. This is the time to share our big thoughts, to bring our greatest ambitions for humanity to the table. This is the time to begin planning and shaping the relationship we will have to one another and to the planet when this crisis has, at long last, passed.

I expect it will be a year or more before we find our way to anything like normalcy and it will not be a return to what we called 'normalcy' before.

Let us create a normalcy, this time, that does not demand perpetual violent conflict, does not pit us against one another, some for survival, others for profit. Let us create a society that does not take daily anti-depressants to function without guilt and buried shame for the insistently competitive and oppressive preconditions of an untenable economic system.

Let us remember that our sense of helplessness, of hopelessness, of depressed paralysis has been trained into us. We have been deliberately put to sleep, deprived of our own intellectual and fully empowered capacity as a culture.

Many of us have craved revolution of one sort or another.

We have an opportunity now. This is the opportunity for a revolution without man-on-man bloodshed. The bloodshed comes on a blameless breeze, from a microscopic foe. No revenge may be enacted.

Begin now to make the changes you wish to make.

The pandemic will kill many, will sicken more. It will change the direction and the sentiment of the population in new and unanticipated ways.

To the best of our ability let us steer those changes toward the good. Let us take this opportunity to forge a greater, stronger human bond through the shared, global crisis.

I have some thoughts.

8. Brody

This is a Manifesto of Radical Optimism.

At This Time

For decades, the scientific community has predicted effects of global warming that have occurred over the past several years. The loss of arctic and Antarctic ice, extreme weather fluctuations, more powerful storms, and coastal flooding all bear out the scientific consensus. Within the next decades we can expect dramatic rises in sea levels, droughts in formerly fertile regions, food and water crises around the globe, climate refugees in the millions, economic losses in the trillions, species extinctions that threaten the food chain, widespread starvation, death, the rapid decline of our modern civilization.

Even as this catastrophic change in climate occurs, those in seats of power, those who could best effect change to mitigate the continued damage to our planet's humanity-sustaining ecosystem present a largely united front in protection of the status quo. A shift from the use of fossil fuels to other forms of energy production, they argue, would be too expensive, too slow, or too late. They say this and they accept campaign contributions from the corporations that profit from the extraction, refinement and sale of those fossil fuels. They work with those corporations to unearth contrarian scientists who can provide false legitimacy to a purported skepticism. This does not stop those leaders in politics, in commerce, and in the fossil fuel industry from seeking to insure themselves heavily against the events they claim not to believe will occur.

Wealth disparity is higher than it has been since the Great Depression. The myth of social mobility holds the impoverished in thrall to an economic system that has never served them. The fairy-tale of the pull-themselves-up-by-the-bootstraps millionaire soothes the desperate into an acceptance of their own circumstance. Surely, they believe, their poverty derives from their own laziness, their own inability to achieve, their own lack of ambition. The wealthy blame the poor for their poverty. The poor tend to blame themselves for their own poverty. They believe themselves responsible because they believe the wealthy to be smarter than they. "If you're so smart, why aren't you rich?" lives as a rhetorical precept so deeply seated in the American psyche that it seems to be based in an underlying truth; in fact, it is an underlying fallacy. Wealth does not come to the smartest or the strongest or most competent. It often comes to the dumbest, most corrupt, weak-minded among us. When it does flow to the hands of someone who has fully and justly and rightly earned it in quantities large enough to make a difference, often it is then handed down to that person's offspring who grow up believing themselves to be smarter than their peers based on the wealth they have inherited. Their peers believe it too. The cycle continues.

Under the stress of perpetual financial precariousness, under the misconception that they are to blame for their own situation, under the constant barrage of media assault on their self-image, their self-confidence, their sense of accomplishment, those most in need of encouragement fall prey to depression and its accompanying paralysis. The belief system perpetuates itself and the individuals sucked into the maelstrom sink deeper beneath the churning surface. They fight a seemingly unbeatable force and believe that they deserve to drown simply because they are underwater.

We have reached a critical moment. Unimaginable change bears down on us. We can feel it. Only generations of ingrained, cultivated passivity prevent us all from racing in every direction, seeking any imaginable solution, pursuing any frantic idea down to its last fading feasibility.

Events on a massive scale, geologic events, climatological, societal, economic, can be perceived only as contrasting snapshots taken over time. We can see ice-cap depletion, but we can't know exactly when it started, how fast it proceeds, or the entirety of all it affects. We observe shifts in the jet stream and we can predict some future shifts, but how does that alter the vast weave of the interlocking ecosystems adapted to regional weather patterns? Wealth consolidates into ever-smaller pools of ownership over decades, infiltrating policy and nobody can be quite sure when in that process we started spiraling away from democratic governance toward oligarchic totalitarianism. Watching such processes, we cannot be certain where we are at any moment in relation to critical tipping points.

Only generations of ingrained nihilism and cultivated devaluation of life could cause so many of us to casually assume that we have passed those tipping points. Humanity at its finest does not deny extant threats on some unthinking gambol along the self-destructive paths. For that path to be so diligently trod, we must realize now we have been unconsciously subjected to a tragic forced march.

Experts in many fields have warned us for decades. Concern about the Greenhouse Effect reached my childish ears as early as 1969, and at four years old I was certainly not the first person the climate scientists talked to about it. Efforts to regulate emissions through legislation were challenged by expensive lobbying groups, demanding that the less-well funded scientists prove the greenhouse effect more than a hypothesis. The scientific community began longitudinal studies to prove the theory and changed the language, referring now to the less vividly clear term, "global warming." The lobbying groups, meanwhile, pushed for reductions in governmental funding for pure science – the kind of science that serves mankind in its quest for knowledge even when there's no financial profit seen in it. Corporatist thinktanks in opposition to regulations attacked the term global warming until that too was replaced, now with the far more innocuous sounding "Climate Change," and with this new branding it felt as though we'd all just heard of it for the first time and couldn't have been expected to think about it any earlier.

Similarly, and simultaneously economists have long seen the dangers in under-regulated capitalism. A pure free market economy naturally tends toward increasing wealth disparity. Untended, Capitalism regresses toward feudalism. Yet the self-serving wielders of wealth find ways to convince the public that serving the wealthy is to serve themselves, ignoring and actively striving to discredit non-partisan experts who continue to be proven correct in their concerns.

Those who can most easily take advantage of the masses if those masses are uneducated seek to undermine the public education system. Reducing funding and respect for public education while pushing educational agendas that will protect and educate only the children of the wealthy, leaves the next generations of the poor and the working class entirely at the mercy of a better-educated, better prepared hoarding class that continues to believe itself smarter than those from whom they have deliberately stolen the skills of critical thinking and revolutionary creativity.

The poison of this mythology has propagated through the lifeblood of this country from its inception. The previous inhabitants of this continent were deemed subhuman savages, their population devastated in an act of genocide, so invading settlers believed themselves smarter than those who lacked weapons to fight them. When people were kidnapped, enslaved, worked to death, those who treated them as inferiors believed themselves smarter as proved by dominance.

They knew better at some level, of course, or they wouldn't have felt it necessary to make it illegal for anyone to teach a slave to read. The exclusion of women from the documents on which this nation was founded also served to create a group that the wealthiest and most powerful could control and from that position of control demean and belittle. The mythology of the dizzy dame took root, the little lady, too emotional to handle the hard truths of the world.

We live with a dark tradition. A tradition that says the downtrodden suffer from some natural inferiority that makes it *impossible* for them to rise. This perceived impossibility then becomes a cudgel with which to continue beating them down. They are too stupid, too emotional, too savage, too *something* to learn, to compete, to vote, to participate, to own land, to get out of the ghetto, to represent the company, to hold office. These beliefs infect the spirit of those who live under their oppression as they do the souls of those who benefit from them. Most of the time they drift below the surface, unrecognized, unseen, woven not into the fabric of our experience but into the comforting lining. We all learn our place without knowing it is what we learn.

In living this way, we all diminish ourselves. Those born to wealth may never learn what it is to care about all of humanity. Those born to the gutter may never learn to feel worthy of the love to which all humanity is entitled. Also, those born to wealth may never feel the worth of love and those born impoverished may never learn to believe that not all of humanity is uncaring. Every blade cuts in both directions and our society is guts-deep in blades.

This manifesto, written in a time of darkness, proposes a radical notion. We can be better.

"It has ever been thus" no longer plays.

A hundred years ago or so, two men figured out how to build a contraption that let them fly. They taught others. Others furthered that technology. Now humans fly. Until the Wright Brothers figured it out, man could not fly. Everybody knew that. Our place was on the ground. Everyone learned their place. People could not fly. Until they could.

Nobody had ever been to the moon. Then some people went. A whole lot of people worked together to do complex mathematics without computers and figured out how. Others built the rocket and the capsule. Someone worked out the formula for the fuel. They got it figured out and they did a thing that had not been done before.

We carry in our pockets more computing power than could fit into a city block forty years ago. Twenty years before that adding machines functioned mechanically rather than electronically.

Humanity's capacity for adaptation and evolution has made us the most successful species on the planet. We have adapted and evolved to become so successful in our reproduction and survival that we have begun to deplete and to overwhelm our host body, the ecosystem in which we live. We see it now. We know it. Working together, figuring it out, doing the math, we have an opportunity to do the next very big thing.

It is easy to panic in the face of impending catastrophe, to say, "There is nothing we can do! Millions of people are going to die." Everybody is going to die. Everybody. We can't get around that. Let's just make sure that we don't all die at once. Let's see if we can figure out how to find our place in nature's complex balance.

Let us reduce the wealth imbalance not out of a sense of *noblesse oblige* but because we can't get everyone working on the incredibly pressing problem of the species' survival when many of our greatest minds are forced to worry about their own individual survival.

Let us treat all humans with respect. We cannot hope to overcome the odds we have stacked against ourselves in a hundred and twenty years of industrial damage unless every mind can rise to its greatest creative potential. Each must add its bit of intuition, talent and skill to the task and know that contribution will be embraced, encouraged and appreciated.

We can do this. We are smart enough as a species, intuitive enough as animals, and we are facing a threat as great as any of those that have driven us toward greatness before. We must do it together because learning how to function as a vast cooperative is part of the action that will allow us to think in terms of collective survival.

When society tells us to remain passive, we must insist on taking action. When popular culture tells us to celebrate stupidity and stare numbly into the flow of entertainment, we must insist on staying focused, remaining sharp. When we are asked to dumb something down, we must instead smarten the student up. We must continue to learn, continue to educate, elevate, enlighten others and seek greater enlightenment for ourselves.

This is the inflection point, the moment at which we decide whether our capacity for evolution and adaptation can outpace our capacity for self-destruction.

People will tell us we cannot change the world. If we take their word for it, they will be correct.

When every droning voice moans of nihilistic defeatism, hope itself becomes a tool of revolution.

Take heart.

Do your best.

Bring others.

Imagine for a moment that we do not live at the end of a short brutal history of war and global degradation. Imagine that we live in the last moments of a specietal adolescence. Imagine that we, each of us, will have the opportunity to see, to influence, and to design the very beginning of our much, much longer history of peace, of excellence, of human decency.

This begins the Manifesto of Radical Optimism.

IMAGINE A FUTURE

Core beliefs drive our actions as individuals and as a culture. An individual's core beliefs come into being organically as part of the maturation process. They are not always productive. Sometimes core beliefs become self-limiting, self-sabotaging, even outright self-destructive in manifestation. The same is true of the core beliefs of cultures, of societies, of civilizations.

Western Civilization, from its earliest ascendance, extrapolated the experience of individuals moving through the life cycle. They assumed that the species, too, would live out a span and then face destruction. In the end, said people of desert places, the world will face fire. In the end, said people of fjords, the world will freeze over. People will be raptured. An angry god will come to raze it all, or a loving god will come to take us to a home we've never seen.

Creatures raising ourselves from a hunt-and-gather sustenance into early agrarianism, barely able to understand the movement of clouds, much less make guesses at the nature of suns and stars, had our first anxiety-inducing glimpse at the possibility of the infinite. We had ten minutes free in the afternoon that our parents had never had and lying on our backs in the grass, we knew that fruit would be plentiful for days. Some of us thought about new ways of weaving branches into containers to collect and carry fruit. Some of us thought about how to count the fruits. Some though, some stumbled into far less practical thoughts. Some of us, these most modern of all people, realized that parents aged and died, and children grew into the world behind. In a horrifying flash, a brief vision of infinite time, stretching off behind and ahead seared itself upon the mortal psyche. In instinctive horror and existential pain, the newly rising sophisticates of the cave-dwelling era, scarred over that brain-branded image and carved all of time to a manageable size. It would end, surely within the next generation or two. Right from the start we planned to end. Soon. Always soon. The Gods would come. The seas would boil. The sky would fall.

So, apocalyptic mythology takes root as a core belief in a society.

Natural disasters, epidemics, severe weather events could lay waste to tribes, to villages, to cities. The Plague, when it swept across Europe, took the lives of at least a third of the population, some estimates say it might have been more than half.

The awareness of the unpredictability and fragility of life further instilled in us a nihilistic certainty that eventually a disaster would come along to cause our extinction as it did the dinosaurs.

It is easier to wrap our heads around "we're all gonna die anyway," than it is to experience the vertiginous possibility of geological time or the even more incredible astronomical time. Our lifetimes flash in a continuous flicker of neural activity that began before we had a word for "rock" and might shine, pulsing and sparking onward down the ages and outward toward the stars forever. We rankle at our insignificance as our great, great, great ancestors did. We imagine always that the end is near, that we will be the generation to see how the story turns out. We carve the future of humanity to fit our mortal calendar. It is easier. It feels safer.

It feels like a lot less responsibility.

These core beliefs, for many, have been codified into doctrine. Religions build this deadline mentality into sacred texts. The very thought of another possibility feels naughty and dangerous, punishable and shameful. People turn off the part of the brain able to think so big a thought, so grand a thought, so flagrantly irreligious a thought as the one that says humanity might be capable of a big enough evolutionary leap to become an immortally represented force in the universe rather than a flash of organic potential doomed from its first breath to a violent end.

From religion to rebel subculture narrative of small press graphic novels to the popular culture of cinema and television, the apocalypse emerges less as a cautionary tale of warning than as an assumption. Zombies roam our screens every night, slowly eating through the brains of the last remnants of a terrified, scattered, diminishing human populace. Angry warbands drive the Australian desert in modified lorries seeing their last memories of water evaporate into mirage. Asteroids tear away our atmosphere. Nuclear winter descends.

We have told ourselves these stories for too long. They no longer serve us.

Humanity has endured disasters and catastrophes. Humanity has endured floods and fires. Humanity has created aqueducts, poisoned itself to madness with lead and mercury and then figured out how to do the aqueduct thing without the lead poisoning madness problem. Humanity has learned to break gravity's grasp and set foot on the moon, send robots to mars and into the space beyond Neptune. Humanity survived the plague and defeated Polio.

We can tell ourselves a new story. During periods of optimism, during the enlightenment for instance and during the progressive period of the late sixties and early seventies when the notion that Peace could be achieved through a simple refusal to engage in warfare, visions of a long future begin to take hold. The imaginary future of Gene Roddenberry's *Star Trek* grew from an idea about a long future that leads us away from the destructive influence of capitalist competition and tribal divisions. When humanity allows itself to imagine an ideal world, it begins to believe in its own potential for longevity as a species.

Radical Optimism proposes that perhaps no apocalypse need occur.

With that, comes all that responsibility we fear, the responsibility we have been encouraged to avoid.

If humanity might continue to live well beyond our brief stay what we leave behind becomes significantly more important. How we behave now, the ideas we extol and ideals we engage may affect the larger human civilization's core beliefs for centuries or millennia to come. It becomes our job to work tirelessly toward the creation of a cooperative, determined, future-gazing cultural consciousness. We must set aside the comforting imaginings of a scorched earth, deathscape assumption. We must take action to create a human relationship to the world around us that allows sustainability even as it looks toward the heavens for spatial expansion.

When the growing species of which you are a member begins to stretch toward the stars, seeking breathing room in the vast vacuum, what behavior will we carry into the greater world? When we encounter others out there in the wild, as European explorers did across the globe, do we wish to befriend and embrace knowing we are not alone, or do we wish to re-enact the genocides committed, the destruction we have chosen in the past?

We have been intuiting these ideas as a society for years but, as all grand ideas must, they started as explorations of individual experience and only now find their way into application for the larger entity. Affirmations, intention setting, and aligning the psyche to the desired path play a key role in the forward-looking self-help industry. Meanwhile, more traditional therapies see an importance in honestly confronting memory and past behavior, rooting out the sources of shame. The therapists identify limiting core beliefs and their origins. Life coaches, sensei, and others provide new ways of constructing our inner landscape moving forward. Using meditations, mantras, physical yogic practices, vision boards or reframing and strategy sessions, they offer an environment in which we imagine a future we want and then use metaphor and mind-hack to align our behavior to the compass of our intention.

Now we must apply these practices to the psyche of the larger body.

We must look back honestly, every country and culture, each tribe and every party. We must acknowledge wrongs we have done, redress those we can. We must recognize the habits of thought, the outward behaviors, all the dark manifestations of our most destructive core beliefs, know whence they came and release them as no longer necessary to our sanity. We must recognize those places that we as a species took the wrong message from a childhood experience and heal those obsolete mythologies.

We do not live in a world of scarcity.

We live in a Universe of abundance.

So, also, we must look forward, finding new core beliefs about human accomplishment, our tremendous adaptability and our indominable creativity, our place in a world so much bigger than the plots of land on the single globe we knew when we imagined scarcity into existence. This species learned to draw fire from wood. This species learned to draw invisible energy from the spinning of turbines by a waterfall. This species learned how to refine available fuel sources into projectiles so powerful and yet so delicately guided that it could overpower our gravity well and set equipment down gently on another planet's surface.

We can do so much when we look toward improvement and accomplishment. We can do so much damage when we wallow in self-pitying paralysis, feeling that the mistakes of the past have ruined everything irreparably. Humanity, we fear, moves toward suicide.

Humanity, though, is us.

We decide our actions. We determine our intentions. We navigate by our ideals. We honor our responsibilities.

This is a Manifesto of Radical Optimism,

DRAMATIC CHANGE

Fear of change resides so deep in our collective unconscious that we would rather deny reality than alter our relationship to it. Denial shows up as the first of the five phases of grief as famously explored by Elisabeth Kubler-Ross and less famously by her cowriter, David Kessler. This model has been expanded outward to cover all manner of grief, from one's own impending death, or the death of a loved one, to encompass a painful breakup or the loss of a job by broad stroke armchair psychiatrists and psychologists since.

We have all known people struck by terrible illnesses. Some go straight to work with doctors and therapies to reverse or mitigate the mortal threat. Others pretend everything is fine until the possibility of treatment has passed or the prognosis worsened to the narrowest of odds.

Our civilization has lived in denial as its sickness has become ever more apparent. Yet the plagues that might destroy us, the environmental poisoning, authoritarian kleptocracy, ignorance, overpopulation, and vestigial tribal animosity continue even as we recognize them as the path to our downfall.

With the reaction to Al Gore's Oscar-winning documentary *An Inconvenient Truth* a few years ago, and the subsequent reticence to act to reverse apparent and accelerating climate change, it becomes clear that as a species we live on a vast spectrum of openness to new ideas and the challenges they present. Some people at one end of the spectrum learn of the danger to life posed by climate change and immediately go to work changing their own habits to better consider the needs of the planet as a whole and become active in striving to push legislation or public awareness, doing all they can to stem the tide. Others, at the far end of the spectrum, so reject and deny the change that even as the predictions of global warming's effects become the reality of today's weather patterns and extinction rates, they hold onto a false hope that the science lies, that the status quo can remain, that things do not fall apart and the center can hold indefinitely.

Our system of governance through democratic representation has become corrupted by money, by outside interference and by ever more hackable voting systems. We know this. Still, very few of us take action to change the fundamental structures we have lived in. Rebuilding a house from the foundation up threatens to be chaotic and unsettling. In the end, though, it beats having the dry rot and termite damage bring the whole thing down while we sit comfortably on our couches pretending the problems do not exist.

The slow growing authoritarian kleptocracy has slowly whittled away at those provisions of the law and the social construct that gave us any semblance of an egalitarian culture. The wealthy have consistently affected the legislation in ways that allowed them to become richer and more in control of the legislation. The legislature has both courted the wealthy for donations and become so wealthy itself that it accelerates this class-dividing system of creating laws to benefit the best-heeled among us. Wealth collects in the hands of the few while the many suffer.

To learn history is to know that the poor can rise up. Wealth disparity will not be corrected by the invisible hand of the marketplace. The rich have no more right to life, liberty and the pursuit of happiness than anyone else. Wealth does not imply intellect or capability or education. To protect themselves from a well-informed public, the wealthy who control the legislature and the legislators who need, envy, and fear the wealthiest ruling class must protect itself from facing an informed public.

The long campaign to keep the workers from thinking for themselves, a grotesque tradition that reaches back to the anti-literacy laws of the four-hundred-year period in which slavery was legal, lives on in today's carefully crafted Charter School initiatives and privatization schemes. Systematically defunding the public education system ensures that nobody who cannot afford private education will develop the critical thinking skills necessary to change their station. Individual intellect derided in favor of athleticism primes the public to disdain learning itself. Those most deeply in sync with this downward trend find ways to subtly celebrate stupidity. A long-running television game show called *Are You Smarter Than a Fifth Grader?* literally made a prize-winning game out the inability of grown, functioning citizens to answer grade-school level questions on topics such as math, geology, geography and civics asked by a charming, southern-accented millionaire.

Ignorance sold as charm becomes a point of pride. Angry xenophobes openly object to bilingualism as if knowing a second language makes a person inferior and worthy of scorn. To undermine faith in science, exchange terms of art for common parlance and meanings until words such as "hypothesis," "theory," "idea," blur together into a general uncertainty. Popular culture turns scientists and professors into objects of ridicule. Heroes become nothing more than tough-guy fist-fighters and the physically powerful.

Comic book heroes, once fodder for childhood fantasies of potency in a big world, now comprise the central figures in a fascist wet dream. A wealthy weapons designer in a suit that makes him strong teams up with other unstoppably powered individuals to protect the poor, the weak, the peaceful from vast imaginary enemies. The strong, by virtue of their strength, must be heroes and therefore can be trusted.

Overpopulation obviously strains our resources. As our medical acumen and advances in nutrition, dwellings, weather-resistant garments and other technologies have extended our lives, we have continued to reproduce at rates that served us well as we emerged as a soft-flesh species in a sharp-tooth world. Now, continued algorithmic expansion serves only those at the top of the capitalist pyramid scheme we call a modern economy. Like any Ponzi scheme, the economic structure on which modern societies are built requires a constant influx of new players always coming in at the bottom. These people, all putting in their small contributions allow the next level up to gather some profit and pass some of that on upward until it gathers in vast quantities at the top of the chain. When those layers of the pyramid depend on product, sales and commerce, what the base really demands is slave labor. A great number of people working hard for barest sustenance keeps this system functioning to the benefit of those at the very top.

At every plateau on this unclimbable structure, the fear of change controls both individuals and entire classes. The fear of losing what one has prevents those at the bottom from making a collective effort to unseat those at the top just as it keeps those at the top constantly fearful of a terrible fall that might occur if those below gain any wealth or education or self-determination.

Still, the structure needs babies, lots of babies, to grow up stupid, to fill the factories uncomplaining, to make the new fidget spinners and to sell the new fidget spinners and to buy the new fidget spinners.

Given an awareness of the dangers we face as a society, we must comfort one another in the knowledge that we all strive to solve the big problems. The big problems, the great wealth disparity, the climatic changes, the overpopulation of our planet, the creeping totalitarianism that brings with it anti-intellectualism, the politics of division, and now a fast-spreading virus will require big solutions. We cannot find incisive, vital, systemic solutions unless we all think creatively. We must develop our critical thinking skills and encourage one another to do the same. We need ideas. We need hypotheses. And when facts prove out our theories, we must be ready to act on those theories until they come to be recognized as laws.

Like cancer patients who change priorities to handle the mortal crisis though it means frightening disruption of a schedule, a plan, a comfortable life, we must now recognize the mortal urgency. Only when we accept that carbon footprints matter will we begin to alter our behaviors. Only when we see that the economic structure we live under is built on our backs and is not sacrosanct can we imagine new ways of distributing resources. Only when we recognize that education, science and intellect can save us can we let go the paralyzing fear that says we are too far along our path to change direction.

The patient is sick. It may not yet be dying.

While we live, we learn. We adapt. We grow. We think. We explore and develop solutions.

Humanity has come through hard times before.

When we allow ourselves to recognize change, we adjust to handle it. When we speak truth to ourselves, we can observe and dismiss our own reluctance to evolve and overcome inertia. We, all of us, share a place in a massive civilization that has found enough hidden energy in rock and in fluid to build cities of steel and glass. Our species has altered landscapes to its liking. We have done great things. We have also made mistakes and done some dreadful damage.

We accomplish magnificent things. We can take the time and put in the effort to fix those things that we have done wrong, to find new ways to do better. Our discomfort with change need not obviate our chances of survival.

This is a Manifesto of Radical Optimism.

AN END TO MILITARISM

Warriorism, the manufacture and use of weapons of ever-increasing destructive power cannot be said to benefit all mankind by any means. Its very intent is to damage some of mankind. We know this. Even the military-industrial magnates know that they cannot try to sell anyone on a pro-war agenda. They mask their market niche, the very core of their business plan, behind euphemisms so as not to acknowledge the true nature of their deadly endeavor. Missiles are called Peacekeepers so that we will not notice they are the product of warmongers. We talk in self-congratulatory terms about the new *stealth* component in our bombers and fighters so we won't have to grapple with what it means that we, as a nation continue to spend money and resources making machines that will allow us to bomb and fight.

Whether we support *Freedom Fighters* or defeat *Terrorists*, whether we *liberate a country* or *protect a legitimate government from an armed insurgency*, the real action is pretty much the same. We use weapons to kill the people we find inconvenient to our national goals in a region.

Since World War Two, the United States and its allies have always been involved in military conflict somewhere in the world. The brief era following our involvement in Viet Nam felt like a respite from this militaristic norm as the peace movement made war unfashionable, but the cold war with the Soviet Union continued through that time. The un-ending war in Korea remained in effect as well. Most importantly, the manufacture of military equipment and the maintenance of a standing army continued unabated.

We remained as committed to war in peacetime as we had become during the conflict. The result was that peace could not last.

A couple of overlapping generations lived under an assumption that militarism had always been a part of the American structure. Jingoistic, almost fetishistic support for the military became a shibboleth for patriotism, the gateway drug to nationalism. In the years after public rejection of the military's actions in Vietnam, the armed forces and their propaganda arms in the media and the pentagon saw to it that any criticism of military adventurism, military missions, military conduct would be seen as criticism of the *troops*, our *brave men and women in uniform*. Thus, any critical thought applied to the actions of the military, to which more than half of our tax money goes, must be shunned. To question the validity of any of the killing done overseas is to disrespect the *sacrifice* of the troops, the grief of the parents, the importance of the mission.

We all sense that somehow the objectives in these deadly endeavors lie more in oil and money than in the freedom for which the government tells us 'we' fight. The proof, though, remains vague, hidden behind a gauze of National Security secrecy and public aversion to being seen as the first one to risk disrespecting the sacrifice of the noble, underpaid, fetishized volunteer force.

Why are teachers not given priority seating on flights? They too choose a profession that serves the nation. They too volunteer to take on a task that pays far less than the skills set required would suggest is appropriate. Hell, Postal workers provide a valuable service for government wages, hard work as a choice. Police and Firemen risk their wellbeing, life and limb in service of others for blue-collar wages. Why do they not receive special treatment at the check-in gate. Can you imagine football games beginning with tributes not to those in uniform whose profession is killing but to those who teach, to scientists, to firefighters, to doctors?

We have so elevated the status of our troops in the eyes of the public that our very ability to imagine peace is impaired. People respond to the notion of evolving beyond war with the dismissive snort that says such ideas do not even bear discussion.

For centuries, though, before the World Wars, Western culture saw long periods of peace in most regions, with wars serving as blood-soaked markers along a timeline. Nations warred intermittently, raising armies when they were needed.

Always war was a means to an end. Now it has become an end in itself, the purpose of expansive manufacturing enterprises.

Always war was fought with the intent of ending war through the defeat of a perceived enemy or the expansion of a border to include that more-defensible rise. Now war continues without pause and we accept that it will not end.

This need not be the case.

If we allow ourselves to believe simply that peace is possible, our view of our future can change. If we imagine a world without war, an economy without weapons manufacturers, a governance built around diplomacy, a society built around civility, truly equal justice, we can begin to see our way toward a civilization that outlives our current crises. When cooperation serves to inspire us rather than competition, we can support one another and build something more beautiful than ever we could in the struggle for individual achievement. What we do together can be greater than what we do in a struggle for superiority, undermining the achievement of those who challenge our own aggrandizement.

Humans are capable of their greatest accomplishments when we work together. Nations excel when we align our efforts to common goals and shared purpose.

The moment we allow our hearts to fill with the sense that our fragile globe is a shared home, not a disputed property, we can act as a species to honor and respect our abode, not as bickering roommates, each waiting for another to do the dishes, to clear the clutter.

We can work together for a long, bright future.

We can serve a common good.

We can be inter-supportive as individuals and as nation-states.

We can leave a history of war behind and become the start of a longer history of peace.

This is a Manifesto of Radical Optimism.

EXPANSION OF CONSCIOUSNESS

A vast number of tribal societies have found substances provided in nature that allow for consciousness expanding experiences. Psilocybin, ayahuasca, peyote, mescaline and more occur in plants around the world. Often used in sacred practices by tribal shaman, they also served in powerful rites of passage guided by the steady hand of the wise men who had gone before. Thus, young people, coming of age, feeling that there was more to the world than their limited perspective allowed, gained the insight, the power, and the expansion of consciousness that assured them that their instinct was correct, that a world greater than their perception existed around them. They gained access to and awareness of the underlying connection between themselves and with the larger world around them, the world of plants and animals, rocks and streams and breezes, all connected, intertwined.

Integral, perhaps, to the peace movement of the late sixties in the United States was the discovery and exploration of the newly created, man-made psychedelic, LSD. Feeling this connection for the first time, unguided and unritualized, young people felt newly enlightened, newly empowered. They discovered and then they realized their power to alter the course of a determined militaristic government through unified, peaceful resistance. This unity of spirit, tenuous at best and certainly short-lived, supported other important social causes of the time. The civil rights movement and women's liberation took shape as long-standing disparities revealed themselves to those so indoctrinated into their normalcy that they had been virtually invisible to all but the most astute observers (and sufferers) of their effects. Long-secret sexual and gender preferences became less shameful and began to ease their way into public awareness and eventual acceptance.

The ritualized drug use that was so common in other, less warlike societies, made the breakdown of imaginary barriers between people a basic element in the education of each new member of the community. When the young people of America discovered the broader perspective offered by hallucinogens, it changed their relationship to one another. It changed their relationship to figures of authority. It changed their perspective on ideas such as national interests, national borders, and the presumed value of violent conflict.

Perhaps it was the lack of such hallucinogenic substances in feudal Europe that allowed its people to travel the globe slaughtering and destroying those more peaceful, communal societies it found while declaring them savages, uncivilized, animal. Surely none who had felt the powerful integration with the greater world revealed through the use of peyote or acid could casually dismiss the humanity of another and kill for the sake of something as petty as worldly possessions or an inflexible belief system.

Perhaps it was the ritual use of such substances that prevented the peoples of the new worlds from developing weapons and military systems to protect themselves. Surely none who had explored the world through ayahuasca-soaked lenses would expect fellow humans to come with such animosity and self-serving intent that they would kill indiscriminately.

The American government and its economically co-dependent military industry recognized – perhaps at an unconscious, instinctive level -- a connection between the drug use of America's youth and the movement that threatened military dominance over the rest of the world and the imagination of the populace. Marijuana use had been vilified since the thirties when its use for paper and fuel production first threatened powerful industries. Now hallucinogens were easy to fold into that established and deeply embedded narrative.

Heroin, originally introduced as a pain killer during World War One -- and named so that its habituated users would be seen as war heroes rather than addicted degenerates – had become a street drug most widely used by African Americans and those Caucasians who lived at the fringe of society.

Any drug not manufactured, patented, and sold by the powerful pharmaceutical companies came to fall under the same generalized disrepute as dangerous, unseemly and probably addictive. Any user of any such drug came to be seen and treated as dangerous, unseemly and potentially criminally violent. The users themselves came to think of themselves as broken, diseased, weak-willed and irrevocably damaged, making the abandonment of self-destructive habits even more difficult to break.

The stories we believe about ourselves hold powerful sway. Even those substances that trigger an awareness of the interconnectedness of all mankind came to make their users feel isolated and separate from the world at large.

Without the ritual aspect of consciousness expanding experiences, without guides who might ease the shock of sudden awareness, young users find themselves abandoned in a world of hypocrisy they fear only they can see. With no aid offered toward the integration of their new insight, they find themselves hoping to put language to their realizations, striving to further crystallize their comprehension and use again, and again until a habit is formed. Told that such habits are unbreakable they begin to believe themselves trapped. Told that addicts remain addicted and irredeemable they sink into spiraling cycles of use and self-recrimination, vilified by those around them as much as they are by themselves.

The tragedy of America's addiction epidemic lies not in its extent, but in its avoidability.

When the consciousness expanding use of drugs is remembered to be not a character weakness but a natural part of the maturation process, we can regain our species' magical ability to see beyond our limited perspective. Only when we allow our minds to embrace the larger whole of which each of us is but a small part, can we truly begin to comprehend the possibility of a species that exists as part of a system. Only when we have the altered awareness that builds respect for the plants and animals all of which depend on one another can we begin to reproduce not as a virus or as cancerous cells on the body terra, but an astoundingly adaptive and evolving element in a magnificent faunascape.

We are a part of something.

We must each learn of the something before we can properly function as individual someones and proper servants to the beautiful whole.

Addiction, though difficult, can be overcome when it can be parsed from self-image, from shame, from character.

It can be made obsolete when the use of experience-altering chemicals can again become a rite of passage, a ritualized exploration, an educational process of discovery that can shape the psyche to see the interconnectedness of mankind, the layers of self-deception required to remain in conflict and competition, and the possibility of a loving, peaceful, cooperative world.

This is a Manifesto of Radical Optimism.

ECONOMIC REALIGNMENT

Wealth disparity grows with each passing year. Governmental administrations that rise from the left and from the right differ largely in their approach to social issues, but all show allegiance to the moneyed minority. Thus, whether those who rise to power come from the Democratic side of the aisle, promising social progress and economic growth for the working and the middle class or from the Republican side of the aisle, promising more regressive and traditionalist social policies and economic growth for the working and the middle class, the entire nation comes to be disappointed in an economic structure that changes only in ways that benefit the investing class.

What was once called "supply side" economics – the erroneous belief that tax breaks for the wealthy and the corporations would spur growth and hiring, and serve everyone within the economy – came to be rebranded as the more easily comprehensible "Trickledown Theory," while remaining no less egregiously misguided. Individuals and corporations with great wealth tend to hoard. Only when hiring and reinvestment proves profitable through savings against high tax rates do these hoarders release their grip on the wealth they've collected and allow it to flow back into the larger economic pool.

Once tax codes began to lean in favor of those at the high end of the Capitalist structure, the tiny minority of entities that controlled the vast majority of the wealth realized that they could use a fraction of their wealth to influence the political structure and inevitably they did so to the benefit of their own profit margins and their hoarders' impulses. The wealthy supported those politicians who would make them wealthier. The politicians happily did the bidding of their biggest donors.

Just as the disproven supply-side economics came to be known as Trickledown Theory, the wealthy oppressors of the workers rebranded themselves as "Job Creators." The idea that government should be small was repeated so many times everybody believed it without wondering if a huge country functions best with a small government. The repeal of banking regulations made it easier for the investing class to hold on to their wealth and their greater wealth allowed them increasing power on the levers of governance.

The loosening of controls on monopolies allowed the media — print, broadcast, entertainment, news, all of them — to fall into the corporate ownership of fewer and fewer entities. With those consolidations, a few relatively like-minded wealth-hoarders took control of the zeitgeist, presenting homogenously comforting distraction. For those who wished to be informed on matters of international affairs, economic policy, science, they offered uninformative carefully crafted performative debate designed to disengage critical thinking mechanisms. Where once intellectuals debated policy, now pundits traded talking points. With each new merger and every reduction in the playing field, the remaining few players increased their influence and of course, their income. Thus, they too gained increasing control in the halls of the capitol, pushing for more freedom to broadcast as they will, to merge as they will, to abrogate any responsibility as powerful vehicles for communication and education in favor of a rapacious desire to keep audiences in thrall to screens and celebrity-worship unchallenged.

With wealth-supporting politicians in place, the Supreme Court came to be stacked with those most sympathetic to the ideology of the legislators and executives who put them in place, so ultimately we came to the "Citizens United" ruling which said that "Money is speech," guaranteeing those with the most money the loudest voice.

This is how unregulated Capitalism slides gravitationally back toward the Feudalism from which it first grew.

Our collective imagination looks at the dangerous interplay of finance in politics and sees the rise of Feudal Moneylords. We are trapped in the Ponzi scheme sold to us for generations under the name Capitalism. Like any pyramid scheme, the only way for those at the top of the ladder to continue gathering income is for the base of the pyramid to grow ever wider, the pool of contributors ever broader. This is the real reason that those most committed to the continued success of the scheme are the most opposed to abortion. Unless the population continues to grow, the base of the pyramid will contract. While insisting that the birth of children matters deeply to them, these same organizations go out of their way to defund proper public education. Those least able to think critically are least likely to recognize themselves as the victims of injustice, and the most invested in the myth of up-by-the-bootstraps class mobility. Without the illusion that competitive hard work leads to financial success people might begin to act in concert and realize that they are being conned.

Anti-trust laws and regulations to prevent monopolization of industries once served to delay the consolidation of capital. Progressive tax rates that took significantly higher percentages of the money earned by the wealthiest people and corporations encouraged reinvestment and dispersal of wealth. Knowing that money from their taxes will benefit everyone, the upper class then seek ways to widen their influence while reducing their tax burden. When it can serve them and keep some of their cash out of the hands of the government, they begin reinvesting in their own businesses. This is when they become *actual* job creators, when they expand and expend knowing that to be the best of use of their profits.

Such a tax structure creates significantly more revenue for the government to use for things that benefit the larger society such as education, the arts and the pure sciences – things that serve mankind in its quest for greater knowledge, greater self-expression and other such communal benefits but guarantee nobody any particular financial profit.

These more progressive tax structures tend to serve society and community rather than serving only those with capital. Fearing challenges to the Capitalist ideal, a free-market economy which has already proven itself to unfairly favor those with Capital, the self-serving wealth-hoarders began finding ways to vilify all other economic structures. While Socialist structures function very well in some of the healthiest and most successful European and Scandinavian countries, only those states in which Socialism has failed or fallen into corruption are ever referenced. Tribal nations all over the world — including the Iroquois Nation on whose inter-tribal agreements much of our constitution was loosely based — managed to survive and indeed to thrive in Communist cooperation, only those modern failed experiments in Communism that drifted into authoritarianism ever come under consideration when one discusses that economic structure. Mention of these other, organically developed forms of Communism are dismissed out of hand as having 'failed' because they fell to a genocide.

These systems did not lead to perpetual expansionism and border conflict. Where nobody owns the land, no borders need be drawn. Such cultures, therefore, tended to invent and advance tools for agriculture and hunting rather than for warfare. Faced with the black-powder and steel weapons of expansionist Feudalism and then Capitalism they succumbed swiftly.

A purely Darwinian Capitalist might say this proves those cultures inferior. Those cultures survived for centuries, though, without destroying their environments, without sabotaging their own water supplies and poisoning their air.

Such efforts have been made to muddy the water, that many in modern, educated America find themselves wholly incapable of distinguishing between the economic systems of Communism and Socialism, the systems of governance called Authoritarianism and

Totalitarianism, and the social power structures known as Oligarchy and Plutocracy. All these ideas, economic, governmental and social blur into a largely homogenous idea known vaguely as "evil," not because they are understood, critiqued and determined to be immoral or damaging to humanity but rather because they are not "Democracy." When Oligarchic manipulators conflate all these ideas, they do not do so to protect the sanctity of Democracy. We know this because willingness to gerrymander, to suppress votes, to advance their agenda in spite of the will of the people betrays a lack of trust in the very mechanism of Democracy, the idea that the will of an informed majority should hold sway. What they protect is Capitalism, the system that most serves them, and worse, *unregulated* Capitalism protected under the name of "freedom" despite the vast number of people it effectively enslaves.

When a person must labor at a demeaning, dehumanizing job in order to meet the basic needs of survival, when a person's spirit bends and eventually breaks under increasingly burdensome financial demands unmet by decreasingly profitable employment is that anything more than slavery? Rent leaves people so broke they must exhaust themselves, filling their days and nights with unending labor to pay for food, for heat, for electricity. They know that any medical or family emergency will require the use of credit forcing them further into debt to the banks that then charge them interest for the privilege of survival. Can they really be said to be anything more than serfs in fealty to their landed lords?

Capitalism can arguably be described as the most successful economic system to date, if we judge success purely by survival and domination over other systems. Certainly, Capitalism has allowed for some great accomplishments, remarkable inventions, technological advancements, and improvements in lifespan, in housing, in myriad aspects of the human experience. It also, arguably, rewards dickishness, allows the selfish to prevail, and turns human decency and a strong moral compass into distinct disadvantages.

Those who most exalt the Capitalist system tend to cite competition as the driving force toward human achievement. In fact, the greatest accomplishments of humanity have come from systems of cooperation. One Egyptian ruler, wanting a bigger burial mound than another, could not build a pyramid. That grandeur required the work of hundreds, thousands of people working together toward the construction. Did competition with the Soviet Union lead to us landing on the moon first? Sure. But both the US and the Soviet space programs were made up of many people working together to accomplish what none of them could alone, what they could not have had they been competing internally rather than cooperating.

Of course, if we judge an economic system by other standards, Capitalism might be the worst. How well does an economic system serve the needs of the many who live under it? How well can an economic system function without requiring the system's adoption by those outside its reach? Does the economic structure depend at its very inception on an untenable state of perpetual growth in all sectors or a dehumanized slave class?

Ideologies, 'isms,' get their labels from their core organizing principals. Just as racism, sexism and ableism organize a set of values based on race, sex and ability respectively (if not respectfully), Capitalism, Socialism, and Communism organize a set of values around the ideas of Capital, Society, and Community.

The idea that "possession is 99% of the law" lays bare the sickness that has taken hold. If laws represent humanity's desire to live by an agreed upon set of rules, why must concepts of property and ownership dominate the conversation rather than humanity and decency?

When socially supportive programs such as the Social Security system, the Welfare program, proposed systems for universal healthcare, the maintenance of roads and bridges and Public Education are derided as Socialist and therefore scorned or threatened with defunding, it is never because they do not function for the betterment of society. Always, someone has seen a way to profit or a way to better secure their own economic holdings by making society less responsive to the needs of those without financial means.

As we take the time and put in the effort to parse out the differences between varying economic, governmental and social structures we find that we can choose not based on a general sense of abhorrence fostered by decades of misinformation, disinformation and branding. We can re-educate ourselves to the possibility of change, of growth, of societal evolution. We can rededicate ourselves to building a society and an economy that raises everyone, incrementally over time.

First, we can see to it that everyone is housed, clothed and fed. When that has been accomplished, we can make certain that every person in our society, in our world has access to health care, physical and mental. We can make electricity and education available to all.

These noble goals, all of them, we can achieve. We must begin by recognizing that we have the responsibility and the capability. We must accept this challenge though it mean relearning, realigning our economic structure to our most compassionate ideals.

We compete at work, we compete in school, and we compete as recreation.

The time has come for a comprehensive reprioritization. It is time to place the person above the property, above the capital. It is time to put the group above the person. It is time to think of society, rather than several reductive tribes. Only when these shifts take place can we begin to value cooperation and all that it accomplishes more than we value competition.

When people work together, we accomplish incredible things.

Let us work together. Let us cooperate to create, to innovate, invent, to rebuild from the foundation upward. Let us find our way together out of a dystopian present into a brighter, more beautiful future.

This is not easy. It is necessary to the freedom to which we have long proclaimed ourselves dedicated.

It begins now.

This is a Manifesto of Radical Optimism.

ALTERNATIVE ENERGY

Nikola Tesla, the man who gave us alternating current and harnessed the power of Niagara Falls to generate electricity, believed that charging money for electricity would be like demanding a royalty be paid to the ancestors of Prometheus every time we lit a match. Surely an energy created naturally through the interactions of elements found in the world around us could not be owned.

Nonetheless, we all pay electric bills.

Let's start with a quick primer on how electricity is generated. A magnet needs to be rotated within a construct of coiled copper wires. That's literally it. If you can find a way to make a rotor spin, you can generate electricity. You can do it with a crank, you can do it by pedaling, you can do it on a large scale using the vast powers of rushing rivers or air currents, the ebb and flow of the ocean, the rising and falling tides or you can do it with a steam engine. It doesn't matter what turns the magnet in the middle, as long as it turns.

Many of us are aware that somehow traditional electrical generating plants contribute to the ongoing deterioration of our biosphere, but we never really wonder why that is. Electricity can be generated by the movement of the air, the capture of sunlight, the flow of water, but humans tend to avoid changes of behavior and technology. There are nearly 1500 power plants in the US that utilize natural gas, 400 that depend on coal and 61 nuclear power plants. These huge devices use heat, whether from burning fossil fuels or from a controlled nuclear reaction, to heat water to run steam engines to turn enormous turbines. As far as we have evolved in our technologies over the past hundred years since the internal combustion engine made individual transportation a hallmark of modernity, the bright cities, mass communications and electronic network of near-sentient devices that make up the internet and the internet-of-things (IOT) all run on electricity generated by steam engines.

The simple logic of childhood tells us that with the ability of humanity to innovate and invent we can find ways of turning those magnets other than the inefficient and pollution-producing process of burning coal to run a steam engine. Surely with the miniaturization of electronics proceeding along the predictions of Moore's Law, now well beyond the point at which nay-sayers believed it would fail, with the intricate and seemingly infinite splitting of bandwidths for private, public and mass communications, with the perpetual expansion of science and engineering's developments in the exploration of space, the examination of atomic and quantum-level causalities, surely *some* true advancement in energy production might have occurred beyond the steam engine.

We know that solar cells and advancements in piezoelectrics show promise. Already wind turbines and water turbines use Earth's own kinetic propensities to bring us power. In a closed, functioning ecosphere, nature provides all that is needed for species, even advancing species to meet their needs if they can remain within the population and consumption limits that allow the system to support them. A closed ecosystem will adapt to a certain amount of overpopulation by any given species, then it will respond defensively and ultimately it will collapse unless a balance comes to be restored.

With human expansion and reproduction overwhelming the sphere, we continue to meet our energy needs utilizing inefficient steam power, produced largely by burning fossil fuels which the planet offers in limited supply. We must find every renewable, non-finite source of energy available to us and we must use each to its greatest efficiency as our knowledge grows and our ability to recognize and utilize energy sources advances.

Remember that in geologic time, it has not been that long since humanity learned to utilize fire rather than fearing it. In the timeline of humanity since then, the discovery of electricity as a manipulable force came incredibly recently. Almost immediately, scientists, trained and amateur, saw potential uses for this newly tamable natural force.

The mind of Nikola Tesla, ill suited to Capitalism, understood at an instinctive level, the mathematics and subtleties of the electric force. Were it not for a car company, many would be wholly unfamiliar with the name of the man who designed the generators at Niagara Falls, creating from the natural rush of a magnificent river, enough power to switch the future from mechanical to electrical power. We remember his partner, Westinghouse, who profited from the endeavor. For the cost of a one-time build and maintenance, those original generators spun the force of the falls into electricity for thousands of homes.

Westinghouse forgot, and we forgot with him, the other thing about powerful energies that Tesla intuited. He intuited it and he implied it when he spoke of electricity and magnetism as being energies Brahman and Vedic. The world gives us magic and magic must be used for the good of all, for the advancement of the whole. When magic is used for personal gain it turns back upon the user. The stories tell us this, stories that long predate our culture of consumption. Were civilizations and cultures that came before the dark ages utilizing energies in ways we have yet to rediscover? Did cultures learn hard lessons and strive to pass them on, or did others simply feel as Tesla did, instinctively, that those powers of the world we learn to harness must be shared? How many new ways might there be to create electricity? How many new energies might there be to make electricity itself obsolete, a steppingstone on the way to even more magnificently abundant forms of unseen energy yet undetected?

Humanity may truly be very near to the beginning of a long and beautiful future, if we can only stop thinking of ourselves as living at the end of a short and brutal history.

We invent and examine by nature when we allow ourselves the freedom to think, to dream, to imagine. When we tinker and think, when we figure out how someone else did it and build on those ideas, we create new possibilities.

Children invent irrigation systems that save villages.

We broke the hold of earth's gravity using graceless, blunt-force physics before we'd put together the first proper microchip.

When science and the arts flourish, when humanity remembers that thinking is joyous, we accomplish beautiful and powerful things. If those who tend to excel find encouragement and support for great ideas, if we allow ourselves to dare imagine great things, new possibilities will present themselves. Surely the great minds and hands of humanity can find in this time of urgency new ways of producing energy, storing energy, utilizing energy more efficiently than we have been. Likely, the oil companies and the electrical monopolies will seek to make any such innovations unprofitable. That's okay. Making them profitable got us into the situation where our greatest forces are controlled by the greedy. As we discover greater forces still, let us all remember that the new magics must be shared, for the good of the many, for the good of the whole.

Humanity will survive. It will advance. The question is merely how far it must regress first.

We are a curious bunch. We will root out all the possibilities presented by our world. We will find new sources of electricity. We will find new forms of energy to harness and explore. I believe it is possible for us to learn from past mistakes as we discover forces that may serve us if we treat them with the respect due all great magics.

This is a Manifesto of Radical Optimism.

A RENAISSANCE COMES AFTER A DARK AGE

We have seen that when an existing power structure grows to depend on the suppression of new scientific knowledge and artistic exploration, a dark age may befall a society.

During the Dark Ages in Europe, the Catholic church imprisoned and killed scientists and thinkers like Copernicus and later Galileo for suggesting that the Earth is a round object moving around the Sun. They felt that this idea, factual though it was, threatened their power. So, they suppressed the information.

Art was allowed only for the betterment of the Church, and some great art was made under those conditions, by a few, well compensated and celebrated artists whose subject matter and treatment pleased the tastes of that collective patron and did not threaten the status quo.

Women who had passed down remedies and practices for nursing the ill, caring for the pregnant, setting bones and curing conditions of the skin and the spirit were accused of witchcraft, silenced, tortured, slain. Druids who had developed complex understandings of astronomy and the powers of language to affect thought and record ideas were hunted for paganism.

Thought was discouraged. Thought was dangerous. After all it was the pursuit of knowledge that led to the fall of man from the grace of the garden. Those who showed natural intellect were pulled into the church, offered the opportunity to learn within the confines and control of the hierarchy. They were given food and an elevated place in society, but they gave up their right to wed and to reproduce. Those most capable of critical, expansive thoughts were pulled out of the future gene pool in a cycle that amounted to anti-intellectualism at a eugenic level.

Most people did not realize they lived through a dark age. Perhaps they thought that now that Rome had fallen, they lived at the peak of Civilization, free to do as they pleased as long as that also pleased the Church who took care of their afterlife needs, and their Feudal Lords who rented them land. The land they rented allowed them to grow crops to feed their Feudal Lords and the Church and if anything remained, their own families. They were, in their fiefdoms, part of the greatest, most advanced time in the history of the world. Also, of course, their ability to assess their condition with any kind of critical or historical perspective was severely limited. The brightest among them, those most adept at learning and thinking were gathered by the Church and taught to read in a place with a blanket and a warm fire. The dumbest of the lot, those strong enough to work hard without giving it much consideration, were encouraged to reproduce and labor endlessly. So, they believed the world had gotten as great as it was going to. They had the wheel, after all. And woven fabric had been around since they were kids and that stuff was amazing. So now it was just about living through the end times and hoping to get picked as one of the good-enough when the final moment came.

The Catholic Church hoarded control over the inspiring beauty of art, the power of music, the loyalty of nations and the impressive grandeur of visually and acoustically magnificent architecture. They had hierarchical communications networks that spanned a continent, maybe a continent and a half.

When the plague came, something happened in the minds of people who had tried to remain small and invisible in the eyes of a judgmental God and his punitive representatives. The illness struck down Lords and Serfs alike, the pious and the defiant, the Christian and the Pagan. It did not come like a Bible story to kill the wicked and spare the kind. It did not come with warnings from the heavens or instructions on how to behave from this point forward. It came with the unstoppable, unassailable force of mathematics and it reminded everyone of the sameness of people beneath the mantle of humanity. It reduced the population by a third, maybe a half. It pushed people self-protectively apart, pushed them into isolations and contemplations.

People alone imagine.

The world emerged from the plague into a renaissance. The literal translation of *Renaissance* from the French: *Relearning*.

This was not, they suddenly realized, the end of everything. They began once again to have a sense of anticipation for things to come. They explored their world again with the eager curiosity that had been denied them for so many generations overlapping back over the centuries.

Be aware, this was truly a *relearning*.

Remember earlier when I brought up the half-remembered stories of Copernicus and Galileo, persecuted prosecutorially for discovering through observation that the round earth might move around a round sun? Archimedes had known the Earth was round about seventeen hundred years earlier. He had figured out a way to damn-near figure its circumference. You knew this once. You learned about Archimedes once. And at a whole different time, you learned about Copernicus and Galileo discovering that the earth was round, that it traveled heliocentrically, not the other way around. You knew which came first. Still, as a culture we blind ourselves in the retelling to the most important part of it. People *knew* the Earth was round. That information, that factual, scientific, observable, provable bit of knowledge was so thoroughly expunged from the mind of man that a whole power structure might rise, dependent on the believe that a flat earth existed at the center of the Universe. Then, when people with eyes and intellect challenged the power structure's insistent refusal to accept presented truth, those people were silenced ruthlessly.

Actual knowledge can be lost. The trajectory of human knowledge and development is not a straight line.

Imagine what was known by those burned for witchcraft, for sorcery, for communing with devils that we have yet to rediscover? What histories and poems and revelations did we lose when the War of the Trees burned the leaf-strung libraries? What magics have we denied ourselves?

Humanity craves advancement as a species. When a power structure becomes cancerous, serving itself rather than the community, it must collapse inward of its own ineptitude.

When intellect, imagination, innovation and conscience wake up from a long sleep, they wake ready to work.

Over the past hundred and fifty years, plunderers of Earth's provisions have risen to power. They hoard and govern the vast magics of the modern world as once the Catholic Church did, but now those magics come from the potential energy in fossil fuels, the communications bandwidths that allow advertisements to interrupt videogames we play on our phones, the mass-media networks that have coopted art for the sale of commercial products.

Knowing their power structure to be threatened by facts, they repress science. The Thomas Edison built a traveling electric chair that killed monkeys to turn public opinion against Alternating Current because it threatened his Direct Current Generation business. Supposedly competing tobacco companies conspired to question, deny and dispute the science of nicotine addiction and the health effects of cigarettes. Advancements in science are discredited, slowed, bought out and abandoned by vast corporations that profit and profiteer on an unsustainable status quo. Important policy decisions are made without regard for science. Facts are abandoned if they do not support the most profitable model.

Recognize that we have been living in a Dark Age once again, lulled to sleep by our entertainments. We have access to a great deal of information and are told, therefor, that we need not learn anything. Simultaneously we are discouraged from doing so, told that it is difficult to distinguish truth from fiction and we are incapable of discerning. Anti-intellectualism has led to a society in which high-ranking politicians casually question the validity of scientifically proven facts after being mis-briefed by representatives of corporate donors that benefit from a denial of reality,

We believe we are the pinnacle of civilization, and certainly we as a nation rank number one in the manufacture and purchase of mugs declaring the owner the World's Best Dad, World's Best Mom and World's Best Doctor, but is that really enough?

What if we are not at the pinnacle at all? What if we have been deep in a global depression, not the economic kind, the emotional kind and we haven't noticed because we've been so entertained and distracted and medicated?

As we retreat into isolation and contemplation to survive a pandemic, we have an opportunity to rediscover our capacity for learning, for research and discovery, for invention and innovation.

We have an opportunity to see the start of the next Renaissance.

When times are darkest, we have the greatest opportunities to cast light.

Capitalism has trained us all to ignore our empathy, to betray our consciences. It is time to relearn.

We are indoctrinated to value self-preservation and self-advancement over kindness and generosity. It is time to relearn.

Keep your head down. You can't change the world. Do your own work. Don't get smart. You can't fight city hall. We have internalized these self-sabotaging phrases as though they are true. They are not truth. It is time to relearn.

We must relearn. We will relearn.

Religions are much like economic ideologies. If they collapse under the weight of truth, they got it wrong, not the facts.

We will emerge from the Dark Age into the next Renaissance, not as the passive observers television has trained us to be, but as participants. We will discover and explore, engage and expand. We will find the solutions to problems we could not even see. We will do the thing that humans do. We will advance to the next stage of our collective lives, again awakened to the improbable potential of an intellectually advancing species.

This is a Manifesto of Radical Optimism.

THE DEATH OF MANY

We can reproduce and expand in numbers well beyond the capacity of our ecosphere to support us. We've proven that.

As Covid-19 spreads around the globe, across the continents, it both reminds us that we are a vulnerable species for all our intellectual abilities. But even if the planet's defenses reduce our population to pre-industrial levels, we must learn from the past and calculate the means to maintain population caps at numbers low enough to sustain our symbiotic place in the food chain.

Like the man in Tom Goodwin's groundbreaking story 'The Cold Equations' (*Astounding Stories*, 1954) we must realize that the universe, weirdly generous in some ways, has no interest in the sentimentalities of its inhabitants. The numbers must work out or whole systems collapse.

This seems a good time in this book about Radical Optimism to remind everyone that everybody dies. Everybody and every living thing.

Facts, nature and math exist in an ether beyond questions of optimism and pessimism.

To see that we all die may be all we need as modern persons to make the leap to the idea of ourselves as mere contributors to a far larger intelligence, an intelligence that has learned to build on its discoveries over time. Our species, a great and brilliant collective, has learned to express thoughts through sound, markings in clay, knotted cords, strung leaves, in script and then in print and then digitally so that ideas can live beyond the memory of those who first shared them, can promulgate outward in time and across a zeitgeist. Our species has cured itself of many diseases, slowed others allowing its members to live longer and contribute more. Some individuals contribute through labor, building structures to protect us from the elements, structures to capture the energy of the wind, of the water, to fulfill the ideas of others who imagined and designed. We are all, quite literally, part of something much bigger than ourselves.

This idea, almost absurd in its obviousness, threatens some of our most strongly held and deeply cherished sentimentalities, though. We idolize the individual, particularly the rugged one. We gaze upon celebrities whose faces we know from youth to old age. We feel that the free will of the individual must be protected from control. Even as we do this, we strive to conform, to adhere to social norms or to alter them to our liking so that our ways will become the conformist norms.

The wise, the learned, the spiritual, the intellectual instructors of artists in academic institutions have spoken at length on the need to abandon the ego.

Still, we cling to the self. We fear death with the same feral instinct that drove us to run, to climb, to build. We see human life as inherently sacred. We see human life as inherently *more* sacred than any other life. Yet for all our broadening perspective as we realize how much we affect the world around us, we have yet to accept that the simple mathematics require as many deaths as lives lest a planet for which we are ideally suited to symbiosis becomes instead a victim of our parasitism. If life is sacred, so must death be.

The cycle complete, healthy, divine in its own evolution promises that we can survive as a species precisely because we do not strive to do so as individuals.

I do not suggest that we all lie down and die. I am not pro-suicide anymore than I am pro-abortion. But I do believe in absolute autonomy, each over our own bodies, each over our own actions.

When people die in exceptionally large numbers due to war or famine, plague or natural disaster, inflection points occur in the development of civilizations. Such inflection points provide opportunity for dramatic change for the good of all or for the entrenchment of limited and limiting power structures.

For decades we have known that a dramatic change must happen, a change of the heart and the spirit of America and of the world. We have developed an awareness, as a species, of our own potential to become viral upon the skin of our planet, to reproduce exponentially, to damage our host and to bring harm to one another in a frantic competition for survival. We have known that the purely imaginary construct of finance and economics has led us onto a dark path. We have lived with the pain and the burden of knowing that something is wrong and not knowing how to fix it. Worse, we have been indoctrinated to believe that everything is exactly as it is meant to be, and that to strive to change it in any substantial way is delusional at best, treasonous at worst.

We have also done our best to avoid and deter the sort of dramatic change that dramatic change requires. While supermarkets have been well stocked and our rent has been paid monthly, while streaming services offer non-stop reruns of our most soothing prime time series, we have shied away from making the difficult decisions that might bring about real change. We fear the catastrophic consequences of following our consciences and our intellects in a society that rewards keeping quiet, doing our jobs and not thinking too much. We ask, "What if we stand up for what's right and refuse to keep participating in a system with which I disagree?" and someone inevitably responds, "Well, that would be the end of everything! The whole of society would fall apart. Do you know how many people would die if we just deconstructed our economic and governmental structure?"

Many people will die in the next few years of Covid-19. People will die far faster than we are used to them dying. This is tragic only at the personal and sentimental level.

At scale, though, the spreading death of the Novel Corona pandemic provides much needed relief to a struggling planet, a reminder that with large changes in behavior we can allow some environmental repairs to begin almost immediately, and an opportunity for us to make those unwieldy and never-convenient changes to the social and economic structures that we know are broken.

In every crisis, unexpected opportunity presents itself.

Everybody dies. Let us make the world better for those who live.

This is a Manifesto of Radical Optimism.

A POST-SCARCITY MENTALITY

Our ancient animal instincts served us well in the early stage of our development. We learned first to find food, then to hunt game and gather food. All that we needed was around, but collecting it took effort and energy. In winter, food became scarce and so we learned to stock against famine and to fear starvation. This memory from long ago of winter famine, of nature's cycle, left a deep imprint. It was an early, important thing we learned, this idea of scarcity.

As humanity has emerged as the intellectual and creative powerhouse of the animal kingdom, we have managed to overcome the cold of winter with architecture and technology. We have learned to grow and distribute food in a way that can virtually eliminate food scarcity for the populace were that chosen as a goal to be achieved.

Sadly, the remnants of that long-obsolete code in the structure of our DNA, largely unexamined, has yet to be expunged. As a result, we continue to behave in response to a long-remembered scarcity that no longer exists.

Fear of that which is wholly imagined or remembered manifests as anxiety.

This presents in myriad ways. In some, it becomes an underlying perpetual worry about the future. In others it triggers overeating and an inability to stop doing so. Some people hoard money and find ways to hold and grow wealth beyond all individual need. They find ways to keep it within their families as though money attaches itself to a bloodline. Others hoard in more recognizably unhealthy ways, collecting belongings until their homes become unbearably cluttered.

Employers use the perpetual, unspoken threat of firing as a means of demanding ever-increasing productivity in exchange for ever-decreasing rewards. They do this to increase a profit margin that continues to soothe the instinctive fear of scarcity. Employees fall prey to these behaviors and provide ever-increasing effort for ever-decreasing standards of living for fear of a sudden job loss, poverty, hunger.

Obviously, we no longer have need in the modern world for anyone to go hungry. We have a problem with food *waste* in America.

The system of commerce we have developed, the competitive Capitalist system to which so many cling, pushes against anything that prevents its natural development. The system, like its creators, strives to evolve toward something more egalitarian.

Capitalism's most insistent adherents, striving to bolster a construct that the species has fully explored, disproven and outgrown, must reconcile two fundamentally conflicting beliefs, both now demonstrably false. First, Capitalism depends on perpetual growth, and so requires unlimited natural resources. Our natural resources might be unlimited over time, if we as a species operated symbiotically as part of an ecosystem, rather than parasitically as a drain on it, but the demands of a consumerist system demand the latter. Secondly, Capitalism depends on an assumption of scarcity, that long-retained instinct that now serves only to trigger irrational compulsions and anxieties. These two ideas when put next to one another present an obvious paradox. We can't have plenty of everything and yet suffer under the yoke of scarcity.

Only an enervating and disheartening regimen of perpetual mental gymnastics allows us all to function in a system that challenges fact, observation, conscience, ambition and critical thought.

The two underlying principles required by this system both turn out to be false. Perhaps the time has come for us to put some real thought into how we might plan and build a society that provides for all and also instills in us, generation upon generation, a sense of abundance. A sense of place in a cooperative endeavor can replace that genetic vestige of scarcity fear with a species-wide knowledge that we are all cared for, parented and parenting, supported and supporting, surviving, inventing and creating in a place that provides all we need if we do not demand also that it fulfill our every desire.

The individual must learn over time to stop thinking only of him/herself, wailing when hungry, tantruming in frustration. We learn to behave for the good of a family, a community, a tribe. A species that seeks to advance, to look forward, must mature beyond the selfish impulses of infancy.

Humanity has the capacity to learn new things and to develop new ways. We have the capacity for peace just as we have the capacity for war. More importantly we have the capacity for choice.

The belief in scarcity serves only those who have more than enough. Those who say, "supplies are limited," and "buy now before they're gone," intuit the power of this fear and utilize it to keep us buying, to keep us wanting, to keep us afraid. We may miss out on a thing we may not need.

The urgency of scarcity must now come to be recognized as a mythology as strong as any and as dangerous as any that is retained beyond its usefulness, distorted for the manipulation of the masses for the benefit of a self-serving power-structure.

When we accept our place as a species among many, functioning by necessity as part of a larger whole, we realize that we live in profound abundance. When this happens, we can advance.

I challenge you to find any human whose accomplishments did not rely on and build upon the accomplishments and efforts of others. Cooperation comes as naturally to humans as competition. We decide which to nurture, which to feed, which to admire and which to engage.

When we mature as a species beyond these long-held, erroneous beliefs about the way in which nature provides, when we abandon this self-sabotaging belief that privation awaits us at a single misstep, we can open our hearts with the breadth of compassion we truly crave, the breadth of love we truly wish to express, the breadth of generosity our collective conscience yearns to express.

We can make this leap from where we stand. We have climbed from naked starvation, up the sheer cliff of survival. Now we stand on solid ground staring back at the cliff, fearing that it might take us. Let us, instead, walk onward, up the easy, grass-lush rise ahead.

We are capable of maturation. We have prepared ourselves. We have enough.

We can now begin a golden age of human cooperation, of global acceptance, empathy and support.

This is a Manifesto of Radical Optimism.

EPIGENETIC TRIGGERING

The science of Epigenetics tells us that while we all have the genetic capacity for a great many different skills sets, physical attributes, mental acuities and so on, only those that are epigenetically triggered will function. This burgeoning field of study suggests that genes may come to default to an 'on' setting or an 'off' setting in just a generation or two. It even appears that genes within an adult may be adjusted epigenetically to turn on or off. As the coding of DNA comes to be fully understood, might it be possible to flip on a switch or combination of switches to unleash the musical potential or the mathematical abilities of an individual?

If we all begin exploring our natural gifts, shedding the shame of exceptionalism, make scenes, think grand thoughts, do grand things, learn new skills and expand our personal libraries of knowledge, humankind may find tremendously creative solutions for complex, seemingly intractable problems. We learned to fly. We learned to escape the gravitational pull of our planet and set dune buggies down on another planet and show us what they saw. We can, if we all feel the impetus of unfettered ambition, overcome the apocalypse itself.

The work of taking up our full potential as individuals and as a species intimidates us. The responsibility, if we really can affect and direct our own evolution, carries tremendous weight. We can bear that weight.

When we learn new things, we become incapable of unlearning them. Once we know that we have agency in the destiny of our species, how can we possibly go back to the passive behavior of a pre-adolescent humanity?

For centuries we considered ourselves so small in relation to our planet that we did not believe we could harm it. We have proven ourselves, in our masses, to be large enough to do just that. Knowing this, we must now fold into our understanding of our selves this knowledge. We must extrapolate the larger lesson:

Humanity is more powerful than it has known.

If we intend — and I contend we should — to survive into the distant future, to explore beyond the known, into space beyond the solar system, beyond even the galaxy, perhaps eventually dimension beyond the universe, we must learn now to do so without overwhelming the systems we visit and explore. We must learn to do so not as conquerors but as participants.

The time for Dominion has passed. We took on the mantle of rulers and discovered that nature will not be ruled. The sense of control served us for a time. We built tremendous structures and systems that may serve generations to come. We created a society and a civilization, but the foundations of those great entities contained flaws so profound that over time they would bring even the most stable of constructs down under the force of entropy.

We have known, as individuals, in our guts that something has been wrong. The discontent, the churning discomfort we have from childhood with hypocrisies and dishonesties of all sorts, stays with us into adulthood, subsumed in the need to engage in those same hypocrisies just to function in the world. The symbolism of paper money, traded without acknowledgement of its inherent lack of value, requires our perpetual commitment lest a complex economic scaffolding collapse beneath its own fiction. The belief in a world in which honesty is rewarded and decency the norm is encouraged in children. We know the world we wish to create. We have been lying about its existence for years, hoping we could wish it into existence. When we realize that these notions, these basic rules, will not profit the individual, we abandon them a bit at a time, until we betray our early ideals in favor of comfort, of luxury, of opulence or we come to resent those who do.

We live at this tipping point. The old systems of economy, of religion, of competition have brought great invention and discovery and advancement; they have also brought destruction, malice and the near reduction of our ecosphere to one that we cannot inhabit.

We will increase in numbers as a species until we experience catastrophe again. This will continue until we begin to behave as a responsible species with a conscience that extends beyond the basic rules of individual conduct. We contain within us the capability. We know this because we imagine it, all of us.

Humankind must muster the courage to expunge long-entrenched habits of thought that grew from the needs of the un-self-aware animals from whom we evolved. We must develop new habits of thought that serve us better as a whole, and a small part of something larger, not just larger than the individual, but larger than the species.

We must each explore inwardly, discover and express abilities and ideas that might help tilt the scales more swiftly. We must each reignite the intellectual curiosity, the imaginative impulse, the child-mind. We must each flip on the switches we learned to turn off in order to function.

When we create art, we explore and deepen our knowledge of the human condition. When we observe the world scientifically, mathematically, when we look at the tiny things close up and the enormous things far away, we explore and deepen our knowledge of the world around us and where we fit into it.

The more we exercise habits of honest exploration, of conscience-awareness, the more we can return to the natural, evolutionary state. This state can be achieved through meditation. It can be achieved through athletic achievement. This state can be achieved through reflection or through creativity. It can be achieved through any activity that demands and supports full commitment of attention and effort.

In this state, this fully relaxed, fully engaged, non-self-conscious state of focused intent, we may affect our own epigenetics. We can turn on those switches.

This proposition is not an easy one, but it is necessary if we are to evolve into a healthy species, a properly adjusted adult species, not a neurotic, destructive, hostile species. As we mature let us mature to be supportive and involved, not invasive and overpowering.

We are, quite literally, all in this together. We know, though we find it hard to accept, that none of us will survive. We live as individuals under the crushing urgency of mortality.

As a species, if we can understand the interdependent nature of the world that birthed us, we can move into a new epoch. We can rise above petty squabbles, warfare, and border disputes. We can cooperate with one another and with the planet whose hospitality we have long abused. We can become the great, kind, warm, generous species we have always imagined ourselves to be. As individuals we are nothing. As a whole we are a God.

Let us be the benevolent, grandparental God we have long thought might live outside of ourselves. Let us be the God of sacrifice and forgiveness that we realized long ago would serve us better than the vengeful and judgmental God we needed as we rose from the stone age.

We can be this thing. We can do this thing.

The world is not ours. We belong to it; we are *of* it.

Let us stop being good children who behave as we have been told to behave. Let us be terrific adults who accept reality and strive to learn and better fulfil our place within it, to support the efforts of the many, to build a future that lasts beyond this dark age, into the New Renaissance that emerges in its wake.

This is our task. This is our challenge.

This is a Manifesto of Radical Optimism.

www.ingramcontent.com/pod-product-compliance
Lightning Source LLC
Chambersburg PA
CBHW011316080526
44587CB00024B/4015